The New Order of Catholic Mass

THE HOLY MASS IN ENGLISH AND LATIN

CATHOLIC LECTORS PRESS

Catholic Lectors Press
3299 Elliot Avenue
Seattle, WA 98109
Washington
USA

CONTENTS

The Introductory Rites

When the people are gathered, the Priest (P:) approaches the altar with the altar servers while the Entrance Chant is sung. When he has arrived at the altar, after making a profound bow with the altar servers, the Priest venerates the altar with a kiss and, if appropriate, incenses the cross and the altar. Then, he goes to the chair.

As the Entrance Chant is concluded, the Priest and the Congregation (C:) , standing, sign themselves with the Sign of the Cross, while the Priest, facing the people, says:

P: In the name of the Father, and of the Son, and of the Holy Spirit.

C: Amen.

P: In nómine Patris, et Fílii, et Spíritus Sancti.

C: Amen.

Then the Priest, extending his hands, greets the people, saying:

P: The grace of our Lord Jesus Christ, and the love of God, and the communion of the Holy Spirit be with you all.

P: Gratia Domini nostri Jesu Christi, et caritas Dei, et communication Santi Spiritus sit cum omnibus vobis

Or:

P: Grace to you and peace from God our Father and the Lord Jesus Christ.

P: Gratia vobis, et pax a Deo Patre nostro, et Domino Jesu Christo.

1

P: The Lord be with you.

(Or a Bishop (B:) says: Peace

be with you).

P: Dóminus vobíscum.

B: Pax vobis.

C: And with your spirit.

C: Et cum spíritu tuo.

THE PENITENTIAL ACT

FORM A

P: Brethren (brothers and sisters), let us acknowledge our sins, and so prepare ourselves to celebrate the sacred mysteries.

P: Fratres, agnoscámus peccáta nostra, ut apti simus ad sacra mystéria celebránda.

A brief pause for silence follows. Then all recite together the formula of general confession:

I confess to almighty God and to you my brothers and sisters, that I have greatly sinned, in my thoughts and in my words, in what I have done and in what I have failed to do,

Confíteor Deo omnipoténti et vobis, fratres, quia peccávi nimis cogitatióne, verbo, ópere et omissióne

And, striking their breast, they say:

Through my fault, through my fault, through my most

mea culpa, mea culpa, mea máxima culpa.

2

grievous fault,

Then they continue:

Therefore I ask blessed Mary ever Virgin, all the Angels and Saints, and you, my brothers and sisters, to pray for me to the Lord our God.

Ideo precor beátam Maríam semper Vírginem, omnes Angelos, et Sanctos, et vos, fratres, oráre pro me ad Dóminum Deum nostrum.

The absolution of the Priest follows:

P: May almighty God have mercy on us, forgive us our sins, and bring us to everlasting life

C: Amen.

P: Misereátur nostri omnípotens Deus et, dimíssis peccátis nostris, perdúcat nos ad vitam ætérnam.

C: Amen.

Or: FORM B

P: Brethren (brothers and sisters), let us acknowledge our sins, and so prepare ourselves to celebrate the sacred mysteries.

P: Fratres, agnoscamus peccata nostra, ut apti simus ad sacra mysteria celebranda.

A brief pause for silence follows. Then

P: Have mercy on us, O Lord.

C: For we have sinned against you.

P: Show us, O Lord, your mercy.

P: Miserere nostri, Domine.

C: Quia peccavimus tibi.

P: Ostende nobis, Domine, misericordiam tuam.

C: And grant us your salvation.

P: May almighty God have mercy on us, forgive us our sins, and bring us to everlasting life.

C: Amen.

C: Et salutare tuum da nobis.

Misereàtur nostri omnìpotens Deus et, dimìssis peccàtis nostris, perdùcat nos ad vitam aetèrnam.

C: Amen.

Or: FORM C

P: Brethren (brothers and sisters), let us acknowledge our sins, and so prepare ourselves to celebrate the sacred mysteries.

P: Fratres, agnoscamus peccata nostra, ut apti simus ad sacra mysteria celebranda.

A brief pause for silence follows.

P: You were sent to heal the contrite of heart: Lord, have mercy.

C: Lord, have mercy.

P: You came to call sinners: Christ, have mercy.

C: Christ, have mercy.

P: You are seated at the right hand of the Father to intercede for us: Lord, have mercy.

C: Lord, have mercy.

P: May almighty God have

P: Qui missus es sanare contritos corde: Kyrie, eleison.

C: Kyrie, eleison.

P: Qui peccatores vocare venisti: Christe eleison.

C: Christe, eleison.

P: Qui ad dexteram Patris sedes, ad interpellandum pro nobis: Kyrie, eleison.

C: Kyrie, eleison.

P: Misereatur nostri

4

mercy on us, forgive us our sins, and bring us to everlasting life.

C: Amen.

omnipotens Deus et, dimissis peccatis nostris, perducat nos ad vitam aeternam.

C: Amen.

THE KYRIE ELEISON

The Kyrie eleison (Lord, have mercy) invocations follow, unless they have just occurred in a formula of the Penitential Act.

P. Lord, have mercy.

C. Lord, have mercy.

P. Christ, have mercy.

C. Christ, have mercy.

P. Lord, have mercy.

C. Lord, have mercy.

P. Kyrie, eleison.

C. Kyrie, eleison.

P. Christe, eleison.

C. Christe, eleison.

P. Kyrie, eleison.

C. Kyrie, eleison.

THE GLORIA

(Omitted during Lent, Advent and Mass for the dead)

Then, when it is prescribed, this hymn is either sung or said:

Glory to God in the highest, and on earth peace to people of good will. We praise you, we bless you, we adore you, we glorify you, we give you thanks for your great glory. Lord God, heavenly King. O

Gloria in excelsis Deo, et in terra pax hominibus bonae voluntatis. Laudamus te, benedicimus te, adoramus te, glorificamus te. Gratias agimus tibi propter magnam gloriam tuam. Domine Deus rex

God, almighty Father. Lord Jesus Christ, Only Begotten Son, Lord God, Lamb of God, Son of the Father, You take away the sins of the world. Have mercy on us; you take away the sins of the world, receive our prayer; You are seated at the right hand of the Father, have mercy on us. For you alone are the Holy One, you alone are the Lord, you alone are the Most High, Jesus Christ, with the Holy Spirit, In the glory of God the Father. Amen.

coelestis, Deus Pater omnipotens. Domine Fili unigenite, Jesu Christe. Domine Deus, Agnus Dei, Filius Patris, Qui tollis peccata mundi, miserere nobis. Qui tollis peccata mundi, suscipe deprecationem nostram. Qui sedes ad dexteram Patris, miserere nobis. Quoniam tu solus Sanctus, tu solus Dominus, tu solus altissimus, Jesu Christe, cum Sancto Spiritu in gloria Dei Patris. Amen.

THE COLLECT (OPENING PRAYER)

P: Let us pray.

P: Oremus.

And all pray in silence with the Priest for a while.
Then the Priest, with hands extended, says the Collect prayer, at
the end of which the people acclaim:

C: Amen.

C: Amen.

The Liturgy of the Word

The Reader (R:) goes to the ambo and reads the First Reading, while all sit and listen. To indicate the end of the reading, the reader acclaims:

R: The word of the Lord.

R: Verbum Domini.

C: Thanks be to God.

C: Deo gratias.

This is followed by the psalmist or cantor who sings or says the Psalm, with the people making the response.

After this, if there is to be a Second Reading, the reader reads it from the ambo, as above. To indicate the end of the reading, the reader acclaims:

R: The word of the Lord.

R: Verbum Domini.

C: Thanks be to God.

C: Deo gratias.

*There follows the **Alleluia**, as the liturgical time requires.*

Meanwhile, if incense is used, the Priest puts some into the thurible. After this, the Deacon (D:) who is to proclaim the Gospel, bowing profoundly before the Priest, asks for the blessing, saying in a low voice:

D: Your blessing, Father.

D: Iube, domne, benedicere.

The Priest says in a low voice:

P: May the Lord be in your heart and on your lips, that you may proclaim His Gospel worthily and well, in the name of the Father and of the Son

P: Dóminus sit in corde tuo et in lábiis tuis, ut digne et competénter annúnties Evangélium suum: in nómine Patris, et Fílii, Spíritus Sancti.

and of the Holy Spirit.

The Deacon signs himself with the Sign of the Cross and replies:

D: Amen.   D: Amen.

If, however, a Deacon is not present, the Priest, bowing before the altar, says quietly:

P: Cleanse my heart and my lips, almighty God, that I may worthily proclaim your holy Gospel.

P: Munda cor meum ac lábia mea, omnípotens Deus, ut sanctum Evangélium tuum digne váleam nuntiáre.

The Deacon, or the Priest, then proceeds to the ambo, accompanied, if appropriate, by altar servers with incense and candles.

P: The Lord be with you.   P: Dóminus vobíscum.

C: And with your spirit.   C: Et cum Spíritu tuo.

The Deacon, or the Priest:

A reading from the holy Gospel according to N.

Lectio sancti Evangélii secundum N.

And, at the same time, he makes the Sign of the Cross on the book and on his forehead, lips, and breast.

C: Glory to you, O Lord.   C: Glória tibi, Dómine.

Then the Deacon, or the Priest, incenses the book, if incense is used, and proclaims the Gospel.

At the end of the Gospel, the Deacon, or the Priest, acclaims:

P: The Gospel of the Lord.   P: Verbum Dómini.

C: Praise to you, Lord Jesus Christ.

C: Laus tibi, Christe.

Then he (the Deacon or the Priest) kisses the book, saying quietly:

P: Through the words of the Gospel may our sins be wiped away.

P: Per evangélica dicta deleántur nostra delícta.

Then follows the Homily, which is to be preached by a Priest or Deacon.

THE CREDO (PROFESSION OF FAITH)

The Nicene Creed

I believe in one God, The Father almighty, Maker of heaven and earth, Of all things visible and invisible. I believe in one Lord Jesus Christ, The Only Begotten Son of God, born of the Father before all ages. God from God, Light from Light, True God from true God, Begotten, not made, Consubstantial with the Father; Through him all things were made. For us men and for our salvation He came down from heaven, And by the Holy Spirit Was incarnate of the Virgin

Credo in unum Deum, Patrem omnipotentem, factorem caeli et terrae, visibilium omnium et invisibilium. Et in unum Dominum Iesum Christum, Filium Dei unigenitum, et ex Patre natum ante omnia saecula. Deum de Deo, lumen de lumine, Deum verum de Deo vero, genitum, non factum, consubstantialem Patri: per quem omnia facta sunt. Qui propter nos homines et propter nostram salute descendit de caelis. Et incarnatus est de Spiritu

Mary, And became man. For our sake He was crucified under Pontius Pilate, He suffered death and was buried, And rose again on the third day In accordance with the Scriptures. He ascended into heaven and is seated At the right hand of the Father. He will come again in glory To judge the living and the dead And his kingdom will have no end. I believe in the Holy Spirit, the Lord, the giver of life, Who proceeds from the Father and the Son, Who with the Father and the Son is adored and glorified, Who has spoken through the prophets. I believe in one, holy, catholic and apostolic Church. I confess one Baptism for the forgiveness of sins And I look forward to the resurrection of the dead And the life of the world to come. Amen.

Sancto ex Maria Virgine, et homo factus est. Crucifixus etiam pro nobis sub Pontio Pilato; passus et sepultus est, et resurrexit tertia die, secundum Scripturas, et ascendit in caelum, sedet ad dexteram Patris. Et iterum venturus est cum gloria, iudicare vivos et mortuos, cuius regni non erit finis. Et in Spiritum Sanctum, Dominum et vivificantem: qui ex Patre Filioque procedit. Qui cum Patre et Filio simul adoratur et conglorificatur: qui locutus est per prophetas. Et unam, sanctam, catholicam et apostolicam Ecclesiam. Confiteor unum baptisma in remissionem peccatorum. Et expecto resurrectionem mortuorum et vitam venturi saeculi. Amen.

The Apostles' Creed

I believe in God, the Father almighty, Creator of heaven and earth, And in Jesus Christ, his only Son, our Lord, Who was conceived by the Holy Spirit, Born of the Virgin Mary, Suffered under Pontius Pilate, Was crucified, died and was buried; He descended into hell; On the third day he rose again from the dead; He ascended into heaven, And is seated at the right hand of God the Father almighty; From there he will come to judge the living and the dead. I believe in the Holy Spirit, The holy Catholic Church, The communion of saints, The forgiveness of sins, The resurrection of the body, And life everlasting. Amen.

Credo in Deum Patrem omnipotentem, Creatorem caeli et terrae. Et in Iesum Christum, Filium eius unicum, Dominum nostrum, qui conceptus est de Spiritu Sancto, natus ex Maria Virgine, passus sub Pontio Pilato, crucifixus, mortuus, et sepultus, descendit ad infernos, tertia die resurrexit a mortuis, ascendit ad caelos, sedet ad dexteram Dei Patris omnipotentis, inde venturus est iudicare vivos et mortuos. Credo in Spiritum Sanctum, sanctam Ecclesiam catholicam, sanctorum communionem, remissionem peccatorum, carnis resurrectionem, vitam aeternam. Amen.

The Liturgy of the Eucharist

The Priest, standing at the altar, takes the paten with the bread and holds it slightly raised above the altar with both hands, saying in a low voice:

P: Blessed are you, Lord God of all creation, for through your goodness we have received the bread we offer you: fruit of the earth and work of human hands, it will become for us the bread of life.

P: Benedictus es, Dómine, Deus univérsi, quia de tua largitáte accépimus panem, quem tibi offérimus, fructum terræ et óperis mánuum hóminum: ex quo nobis fiet panis vitæ.

Then he places the paten with the bread on the corporal.

The people may acclaim:

C: Blessed be God for ever.

C: Benedíctus Deus in sǽcula.

The Priest, pours wine and a little water into the chalice, saying quietly:

P: By the mystery of this water and wine, may we come to share in the divinity of Christ who humbled himself to share in our humanity.

P: Per huius aquæ et vini mystérium eius efficiámur divinitátis consórtes, qui humanitátis nostræ fíeri dignátus est párticeps.

The Priest then takes the chalice and holds it slightly raised above the altar with both hands, saying in a low voice:

P: Blessed are you, Lord God of all creation, for through

P: Benedíctus es, Dómine, Deus univérsi, quia de tua

your goodness we have received the wine we offer you: fruit of the vine and work of human hands, it will become our spiritual drink.

largitáte accépimus vinum, quod tibi offérimus, fructum vitis et óperis mánuum hóminum, ex quo nobis fiet potus spiritális.

Then he places the chalice on the corporal.

C: Blessed be God for ever.

C: Benedíctus Deus in sǽcula.

After this, the Priest, bowing profoundly, says quietly:

P: With humble spirit and contrite heart may we be accepted by you, O Lord, and may our sacrifice in your sight this day be pleasing to you, Lord God.

P: In spíritu humilitátis et in ánimo contríto suscipiámur a te, Dómine; et sic fiat sacrifícium nostrum in conspéctu tuo hódie. ut pláceat tibi, Dómine Deus.

Then the Priest, standing at the side of the altar, washes his hands, saying quietly:

P: Wash me, O Lord, from my iniquity and cleanse me from my sin.

P: Lava me, Dómine, ab iniquitáte mea, et a peccáto meo munda me.

Standing at the middle of the altar, facing the people, extending and then joining his hands, he says:

P: Pray, brethren (brothers and sisters), that my sacrifice and yours may be acceptable to God, the almighty Father.

P: Oráte, fratres: ut meum ac vestrum sacrifícium acceptábile fiat apud Deum Patrem omnipoténtem.

The people rise and reply:

C: May the Lord accept the sacrifice at your hands for the praise and glory of his name, for our good and the good of all his holy Church.

C: Suscípiat Dóminus sacrifícium de mánibus tuis ad laudem et glóriam nóminis sui, ad utilitátem quoque nostrum totiúsque Ecclésiæ suæ sanctæ.

Then the Priest, with hands extended, says the Prayer over the Gifts, at the end of which the people acclaim:

C: Amen.

C: Amen.

EUCHARISTIC PRAYER I

(The Roman Canon)

P: The Lord be with you.

P: Dóminus vobíscum.

C: And with your spirit.

C: Et cum spíritu tuo.

P: Lift up your hearts.

P: Sursum corda.

C: We lift them up to the Lord.

C: Habémus ad Dóminum.

P: Let us give thanks to the Lord our God.

P: Grátias agámus Dómino Deo nostro.

C: It is right and just.

C: Dignum et iustum est.

Then follows the Preface to be used in accord with the rubrics, which concludes:

Holy, Holy, Holy Lord God of hosts. Heaven and earth are full of your glory. Hosanna in the highest. Blessed is he who comes in the name of the Lord.

Sanctus, Sanctus, Sanctus Dóminus Deus Sabaóth. Pleni sunt caeli et terra glória tua. Hosánna in excélsis. Benedíctus qui venit in nómine Dómini.

Hosanna in the highest.

Hosánna in excélsis.

The Priest, with hands extended, says:

P: To you, therefore, most merciful Father, we make humble prayer and petition through Jesus Christ, your Son, our Lord:

P: Te ígitur, clementíssime Pater, per Iesum Christum, Fílium tuum, Dóminum nostrum, súpplices rogámus ac pétimus,

He joins his hands and says

P: that you accept

P: uti accépta hábeas

He makes the Sign of the Cross once over the bread and chalice together, saying:

P: and bless these gifts, these offerings, these holy and unblemished sacrifices,

P: et benedícas haec dona, haec múnera, haec sancta sacrifícia illibáta,

With hands extended, he continues:

P: which we offer you firstly for your holy catholic Church. Be pleased to grant her peace, to guard, unite and govern her throughout the whole world, together with your servant N. our Pope and N. our Bishop, and all those who, holding to the truth, hand on the catholic and apostolic faith.

P: in primis, quae tibi offérimus pro Ecclésia tua sancta cathólica: quam pacificáre, custodíre, adunáre et régere dignéris toto orbe terrárum: una cum fámulo tuo Papa nostro N. et Antístite nostro N. et ómnibus orthodóxis atque cathólicae et apostólicae fídei cultóribus.

Commemoration of the Living

P: Remember, Lord, your
servants N. and N.

P: Meménto, Dómine,
famulórum famularúmque
tuárum N. et N.

The Priest joins his hands and prays briefly for those for whom he intends to pray. Then, with hands extended, he continues:

P: and all gathered here, whose faith and devotion are known to you. For them, we offer you this sacrifice of praise or they offer it for themselves and all who are dear to them: for the redemption of their souls, in hope of health and well-being, and paying their homage to you, the eternal God, living and true.

P: et ómnium circumstántium, quorum tibi fides cógnita est et nota devótio, pro quibus tibi offérimus: vel qui tibi ófferunt hoc sacrifícium laudis, pro se suísque ómnibus: pro redemptióne animárum suárum, pro spe salútis et incolumitátis suae: tibíque reddunt vota sua aetérno Deo, vivo et vero.

In communion with those whose memory we venerate, especially the glorious ever-Virgin Mary, Mother of our God and Lord, Jesus Christ, and blessed Joseph, her Spouse, your blessed Apostles and Martyrs, Peter and Paul, Andrew, (James, John,

Communicántes, et memóriam venerántes, in primis gloriósae semper Vírginis Maríae, Genetrícis Dei et Dómini nostri Iesu Christi: sed et beáti Ioseph, eiúsdem Vírginis Sponsi, et beatórum Apostolórum ac Mártyrum tuórum, Petri et Pauli,

16

Thomas, James, Philip, Bartholomew, Matthew, Simon and Jude; Linus, Cletus, Clement, Sixtus, Cornelius, Cyprian, Lawrence, Chrysogonus, John and Paul, Cosmas and Damian) and all your Saints; we ask that through their merits and prayers, in all things we may be defended by your protecting help. (Through Christ our Lord. Amen.)

Andréae, (Iacóbi, Ioánnis, Thomae, Iacóbi, Philíppi, Bartholomaei, Matthaei, Simónis et Thaddaei: Lini, Cleti, Cleméntis, Xysti, Cornélii, Cypriáni, Lauréntii, Chrysógoni, Ioánnis et Pauli, Cosmae et Damiáni) et ómnium Sanctórum tuórum; quorum méritis precibúsque concédas, ut in ómnibus protectiónis tuae muniámur auxílio. (Per Christum Dóminum nostrum. Amen.)

With hands extended, the Priest continues:

P: Therefore, Lord, we pray: graciously accept this oblation of our service, that of your whole family; order our days in your peace, and command that we be delivered from eternal damnation and counted among the flock of those you have chosen. (Through Christ our Lord. Amen.)

P: Hanc ígitur oblatiónem servitútis nostrae, sed et cunctae famíliae tuae, quaesumus, Dómine, ut placátus accípias: diésque nostros in tua pace dispónas, atque ab aetérna damnatióne nos éripi et in electórum tuórum iúbeas grege numerári. (Per Christum Dóminum nostrum. Amen.)

Holding his hands extended over the offerings, he says:

P: Be pleased, O God, we pray, to bless, acknowledge, and approve this offering in every respect; make it spiritual and acceptable, so that it may become for us the Body and Blood of your most beloved Son, our Lord Jesus Christ.

P: Quam oblatiónem tu, Deus, in ómnibus, quaesumus, benedíctam, adscríptam, ratam, rationábilem, acceptabilémque fácere dignéris: ut nobis Corpus et Sanguis fiat dilectíssimi Fílii tui, Dómini nostri Iesu Christi.

He joins his hands.

P: On the day before he was to suffer,

P: Qui, prídie quam paterétur,

He takes the bread and, holding it slightly raised above the altar, continues:

P: he took bread in his holy and venerable hands, and with eyes raised to heaven to you, O God, his almighty Father, giving you thanks, he said the blessing, broke the bread and gave it to his disciples, saying:

P: accépit panem in sanctas ac venerábiles manus suas, et elevátis óculis in caelum ad te Deum Patrem suum omnipoténtem, tibi grátias agens benedíxit, fregit, dedítque discípulis suis, dicens:

He bows slightly.

P: TAKE THIS, ALL OF YOU, AND EAT OF IT, FOR THIS IS MY BODY, WHICH WILL BE GIVEN UP FOR YOU.

P: ACCÍPITE ET MANDUCÁTE EX HOC OMNES: HOC EST ENIM CORPUS MEUM, QUOD PRO

VOBIS TRADÉTUR.

He shows the consecrated host to the people, places it again on the paten, and genuflects in adoration.

After this, the Priest continues:

P: In a similar way, when supper was ended,

P: Símili modo, postquam cenátum est,

He takes the chalice and, holding it slightly raised above the altar, continues:

P: he took this precious chalice in his holy and venerable hands, and once more giving you thanks, he said the blessing and gave the chalice to his disciples, saying:

P: accípiens et hunc praeclárum cálicem in sanctas ac venerábiles manus suas, item tibi grátias agens benedíxit, dedítque discípulis suis, dicens:

He bows slightly.

P: TAKE THIS, ALL OF YOU, AND DRINK FROM IT, FOR THIS IS THE CHALICE OF MY BLOOD, THE BLOOD OF THE NEW AND ETERNAL COVENANT, WHICH WILL BE POURED OUT FOR YOU AND FOR MANY FOR THE FORGIVENESS OF SINS. DO THIS IN MEMORY OF ME.

P: ACCÍPITE ET BÍBITE EX EO OMNES: HIC EST ENIM CALIX SÁNGUINIS MEI NOVI ET AETÉRNI TESTAMÉNTI, QUI PRO VOBIS ET PRO MULTIS EFFUNDÉTUR IN REMISSIÓNEM PECCATÓRUM. HOC FÁCITE IN MEAM

COMMEMORATIÓNEM.

He shows the chalice to the people, places it on the corporal, and genuflects in adoration.

Then he says:

P: The mystery of faith.

C: We proclaim your Death, O Lord, and profess your Resurrection until you come again.

Or:

When we eat this Bread and drink this Cup, we proclaim your Death, O Lord, until you come again.

Or:

Save us, Savior of the world, for by your Cross and Resurrection you have set us free.

P: Mystérium fídei.

C: Mortem tuam annuntiámus, Dómine, et tuam resurrectiónem confitémur, donec vénias.

Vel:

Quotiescúmque manducámus panem hunc et cálicem bíbimus, mortem tuam annuntiámus, Dómine, donec vénias.

Vel:

Salvátor mundi, salva nos, qui per crucem et resurrectiónem tuam liberásti nos.

Then the Priest, with hands extended, says:

P: Therefore, O Lord, as we celebrate the memorial of the blessed Passion, the Resurrection from the dead, and the glorious

P: Unde et mémores, Dómine, nos servi tui, sed et plebs tua sancta, eiúsdem Christi, Fílii tui, Dómini nostri, tam beátae

Ascension into heaven of Christ, your Son, our Lord, we, your servants and your holy people, offer to your glorious majesty from the gifts that you have given us, this pure victim, this holy victim, this spotless victim, the holy Bread of eternal life and the Chalice of everlasting salvation.

passiónis, necnon et ab ínferis resurrectiónis, sed et in caelos gloriósae ascensiónis: offérimus praeclárae maiestáti tuae de tuis donis ac datis hóstiam puram, hóstiam sanctam, hóstiam immaculátam, Panem sanctum vitae aetérnae et Cálicem salútis perpétuae.

Be pleased to look upon these offerings with a serene and kindly countenance, and to accept them, as once you were pleased to accept the gifts of your servant Abel the just, the sacrifice of Abraham, our father in faith, and the offering of your high priest Melchizedek, a holy sacrifice, a spotless victim.

Supra quae propítio ac seréno vultu respícere dignéris: et accépta habére, sícuti accépta habére dignátus es múnera púeri tui iusti Abel, et sacrifícium Patriárchae nostri Abrahae, et quod tibi óbtulit summus sacérdos tuus Melchísedech, sanctum sacrifícium, immaculátam hóstiam.

Bowing, with hands joined, he continues:

P: In humble prayer we ask you, almighty God: command that these gifts be borne by the hands

P: Súpplices te rogámus, omnípotens Deus: iube haec perférri per manus sancti Angeli

of your holy Angel to your altar on high in the sight of your divine majesty, so that all of us, who through this participation at the altar receive the most holy Body and Blood of your Son,

tui in sublíme altáre tuum, in conspéctu divínae maiestátis tuae; ut, quotquot ex hac altáris participatióne sacrosánctum Fílii tui Corpus et Sánguinem sumpsérimus,

He stands upright again and signs himself with the Sign of the Cross, saying:

P: may be filled with every grace and heavenly blessing. (Through Christ our Lord. Amen.)

P: omni benedictióne caelésti et grátia repleámur. (Per Christum Dóminum nostrum. Amen.)

Commemoration of the Dead

With hands extended, the Priest says:

P: Remember also, Lord, your servants N. and N., who have gone before us with the sign of faith and rest in the sleep of peace.

P: Meménto étiam, Dómine, famulórum famularúmque tuárum N. et N., qui nos praecessérunt cum signo fídei, et dórmiunt in somno pacis.

He joins his hands and prays briefly for those who have died and for whom he intends to pray. Then, with hands extended, he continues:

P: Grant them, O Lord, we pray, and all who sleep in Christ, a place of refreshment, light and peace. (Through Christ our Lord. Amen.)

P: Ipsis, Dómine, et ómnibus in Christo quiescéntibus, locum refrigérii, lucis et pacis, ut indúlgeas, deprecámur. (Per Christum Dóminum nostrum.

Amen.)

He strikes his breast with his right hand, saying:

P: To us, also, your servants, who, though sinners,

P: Nobis quoque peccatóribus fámulis tuis,

And, with hands extended, he continues:

hope in your abundant mercies, graciously grant some share and fellowship with your holy Apostles and Martyrs: with John the Baptist, Stephen, Matthias, Barnabas, (Ignatius, Alexander, Marcellinus, Peter, Felicity, Perpetua, Agatha, Lucy, Agnes, Cecilia, Anastasia) and all your Saints; admit us, we beseech you, into their company, not weighing our merits, but granting us your pardon, through Christ our Lord.

de multitúdine miseratiónum tuárum sperántibus, partem áliquam et societátem donáre dignéris cum tuis sanctis Apóstolis et Martyribus: cum Ioánne, Stéphano, Matthía, Bárnaba, (Ignátio, Alexándro, Marcellíno, Petro, Felicitáte, Perpétua, Agatha, Lúcia, Agnéte, Caecília, Anastásia) et ómnibus Sanctis tuis: intra quorum nos consórtium, non aestimátor mériti, sed véniae, quaesumus, largítor admítte. Per Christum Dóminum nostrum.

And he continues:

P: Through whom you continue to make all these good things, O Lord; you sanctify them, fill them with life, bless them, and

P: Per quem haec ómnia, Dómine, semper bona creas, sanctíficas, vivíficas, benedícis, et praestas nobis.

23

bestow them upon us.

He takes the chalice and the paten with the host and, raising both, he says:

P: Through him, and with him, and in him, O God, almighty Father, in the unity of the Holy Spirit, all glory and honor is yours, for ever and ever.

C: Amen.

P: Per ipsum, et cum ipso, et in ipso, est tibi Deo Patri omnipoténti, in unitáte Spíritus Sancti, omnis honor et glória per ómnia saecula saeculórum.

C: Amen.

Then follows the Communion Rite

EUCHARISTIC PRAYER II

P: The Lord be with you.

C: And with your spirit.

P: Lift up your hearts.

C: We lift them up to the Lord.

P: Let us give thanks to the Lord our God.

C: It is right and just.

P: It is truly right and just, our duty and our salvation, always and everywhere to give you thanks, Father most holy, through your beloved Son, Jesus Christ, your Word through

P: Dóminus vobíscum.

C: Et cum spíritu tuo.

P: Sursum corda.

C: Habémus ad Dóminum.

P: Grátias agámus Dómino Deo nostro.

C: Dignum et iustum est.

P: Vere dignum et iustum est, aequum et salutáre, nos tibi, sancte Pater, semper et ubíque grátias ágere per Fílium dilectiónis tuae Iesum Christum, Verbum tuum per quod cuncta

whom you made all things,
whom you sent as our Savior and
Redeemer, incarnate by the Holy
Spirit and born of the Virgin.
Fulfilling your will and gaining
for you a holy people, he
stretched out his hands as he
endured his Passion, so as to
break the bonds of death and
manifest the resurrection. And
so, with the Angels and all the
Saints we declare your glory, as
with one voice we acclaim:

Holy, Holy, Holy Lord God of
hosts. Heaven and earth are full
of your glory. Hosanna in the
highest. Blessed is he who
comes in the name of the Lord.
Hosanna in the highest.

fecísti: quem misísti nobis
Salvatórem et Redemptórem,
incarnátum de Spíritu Sancto et
ex Vírgine natum. Qui
voluntátem tuam adímplens et
pópulum tibi sanctum acquírens
exténdit manus cum paterétur, ut
mortem sólveret et
resurrectiónem manifestáret. Et
ídeo cum Angelis et ómnibus
Sanctis glóriam tuam
praedicámus, una voce dicéntes:

Sanctus, Sanctus, Sanctus
Dóminus Deus Sábaoth. Pleni
sunt caeli et terra glória tua.
Hosánna in excélsis. Benedíctus
qui venit in nómine Dómini.
Hosánna in excélsis.

The Priest, with hands extended, says:

P: You are indeed Holy, O Lord,
the fount of all holiness.

P: Vere Sanctus es, Dómine,
fons omnis sanctitátis.

He joins his hands and, holding them extended over the offerings,
says:

P: Make holy, therefore, these

P: Haec ergo dona, quaesumus,

gifts, we pray, by sending down your Spirit upon them like the dewfall,

Spíritus tui rore sanctífica,

He joins his hands and makes the Sign of the Cross once over the bread and the chalice together, saying:

P: so that they may become for us the Body and Blood of our Lord Jesus Christ.

P: ut nobis Corpus et Sanguis fiant Dómini nostri Iesu Christi.

He joins his hands.

P: At the time he was betrayed and entered willingly into his Passion,

P: Qui cum Passióni voluntárie traderétur,

He takes the bread and, holding it slightly raised above the altar, continues:

P: he took bread and, giving thanks, broke it, and gave it to his disciples, saying:

P: accépit panem et grátias agens fregit, dedítque discípulis suis, dicens:

He bows slightly.

P: TAKE THIS, ALL OF YOU, AND EAT OF IT, FOR THIS IS MY BODY, WHICH WILL BE GIVEN UP FOR YOU.

P: ACCÍPITE ET MANDUCÁTE EX HOC OMNES: HOC EST ENIM CORPUS MEUM, QUOD PRO VOBIS TRADÉTUR.

He shows the consecrated host to the people, places it again on the paten, and genuflects in adoration.

After this, he continues:

P: In a similar way, when supper was ended,

P: Símili modo, postquam cenátum est,

He takes the chalice and, holding it slightly raised above the altar, continues:

P: he took the chalice and, once more giving thanks, he gave it to his disciples, saying:

P: accípiens et cálicem íterum tibi grátias agens dedit discípulis suis, dicens:

He bows slightly.

P: TAKE THIS, ALL OF YOU, AND DRINK FROM IT, FOR THIS IS THE CHALICE OF MY BLOOD, THE BLOOD OF THE NEW AND ETERNAL COVENANT, WHICH WILL BE POURED OUT FOR YOU AND FOR MANY FOR THE FORGIVENESS OF SINS. DO THIS IN MEMORY OF ME.

P: ACCÍPITE ET BÍBITE EX EO OMNES: HIC EST ENIM CALIX SÁNGUINIS MEI NOVI ET AETÉRNI TESTAMÉNTI, QUI PRO VOBIS ET PRO MULTIS EFFUNDÉTUR IN REMISSIÓN E M PECCATÓRUM. HOC FÁCITE IN MEAM COMMEMORATIÓNEM.

He shows the chalice to the people, places it on the corporal, and genuflects in adoration.

Then he says:

P: The mystery of faith.

P: Mystérium fídei.

C: We proclaim your Death,

C: Mortem tuam annuntiámus,

O Lord, and profess your Resurrection until you come again.

Or:

When we eat this Bread and drink this Cup, we proclaim your Death, O Lord, until you come again.

Or:

Save us, Savior of the world, for by your Cross and Resurrection you have set us free.

Then the Priest, with hands extended, says:

P: Therefore, as we celebrate the memorial of his Death and Resurrection, we offer you, Lord, the Bread of life and the Chalice of salvation, giving thanks that you have held us worthy to be in your presence and minister to you.

Humbly we pray that, partaking

Dómine, et tuam resurrectiónem confitémur, donec vénias.

Vel:

Quotiescúmque manducámus panem hunc et cálicem bíbimus, mortem tuam annuntiámus, Dómine, donec vénias.

Vel:

Salvátor mundi, salva nos, qui per crucem et resurrectiónem tuam liberásti nos.

P: Mémores ígitur mortis et resurrectiónis eius, tibi, Dómine, panem vitae et cálicem salútis offérimus, grátias agéntes quia nos dignos habuísti astáre coram te et tibi ministráre.

Et súpplices deprecámur ut

of the Body and Blood of Christ, we may be gathered into one by the Holy Spirit.

Córporis et Sánguinis Christi partícipes a Spíritu Sancto congregémur in unum.

Remember, Lord, your Church, spread throughout the world, and bring her to the fullness of charity, together with N. our Pope and N. our Bishop, and all the clergy.

Recordáre, Dómine, Ecclésiae tuae toto orbe diffúsae, ut eam in caritáte perfícias una cum Papa nostro N. et Epíscopo nostro N. et univérso clero.

Remember also our brothers and sisters who have fallen asleep in the hope of the resurrection, and all who have died in your mercy: welcome them into the light of your face.

Meménto étiam fratrum nostrórum, qui in spe resurrectiónis dormiérunt, omniúmque in tua miseratióne defunctórum, et eos in lumen vultus tui admítte.

Have mercy on us all, we pray, that with the Blessed Virgin Mary, Mother of God, with the blessed Apostles, and all the Saints who have pleased you throughout the ages, we may merit to be coheirs to eternal life,

Omnium nostrum, quaesumus, miserére, ut cum beáta Dei Genetríce Vírgine María, beáto Ioseph, eius Sponso, beátis Apóstolis et ómnibus Sanctis, qui tibi a saeculo placuérunt, aetérnae vitae mereámur esse

and may praise and glorify you through your Son, Jesus Christ.

consórtes, et te laudémus et glorificémus per Fílium tuum Iesum Christum.

He takes the chalice and the paten with the host and, raising both, he says:

P: Through him, and with him, and in him, O God, almighty Father, in the unity of the Holy Spirit, all glory and honor is yours, for ever and ever.

C: Amen.

P: Per ipsum, et cum ipso, et in ipso, est tibi Deo Patri omnipoténti, in unitáte Spíritus Sancti, omnis honor et glória per ómnia saecula saeculórum.

C: Amen.

Then follows the Communion Rite

EUCHARISTIC PRAYER III

P: The Lord be with you.

C: And with your spirit.

P: Lift up your hearts.

C: We lift them up to the Lord.

P: Let us give thanks to the Lord our God.

C: It is right and just.

P: Dóminus vobíscum.

C: Et cum spíritu tuo.

P: Sursum corda.

C: Habémus ad Dóminum.

P: Grátias agámus Dómino Deo nostro.

C: Dignum et iustum est.

Then follows the Preface to be used in accord with the rubrics, which concludes:

Holy, Holy, Holy Lord God of hosts. Heaven and earth are full

Sanctus, Sanctus, Sanctus Dóminus Deus Sábaoth. Pleni

of your glory. Hosanna in the
highest. Blessed is he who
comes in the name of the Lord.
Hosanna in the highest.

sunt caeli et terra glória tua.
Hosánna in excélsis. Benedíctus
qui venit in nómine Dómini.
Hosánna in excélsis.

The Priest, with hands extended, says:

P: You are indeed Holy,
O Lord, and all you have created
rightly gives you praise, for
through your Son our Lord Jesus
Christ, by the power and
working of the Holy Spirit, you
give life to all things and make
them holy, and you never cease
to gather a people to yourself, so
that from the rising of the sun to
its setting a pure sacrifice may
be offered to your name.

P: Vere Sanctus es, Domine, et
merito te laudat omnis a te
condita creatura, quia per Filium
tuum, Dominum nostrum Iesum
Christum, Spiritus Sancti
operante virtute, vivificas et
sanctificas universa, et populum
tibi congregare non desinis, ut a
solis ortu usque ad occasum
oblatio munda offeratur nomini
tuo.

He joins his hands and, holding them extended over the offerings, says:

P: Therefore, O Lord, we
humbly implore you: by the
same Spirit graciously make
holy these gifts we have brought
to you for consecration,

P: Supplices ergo te, Domine,
deprecamur, ut haec munera,
quae tibi sacranda detulimus,
eodem Spiritu sanctificare
digneris,

He joins his hands and makes the Sign of the Cross once over the bread and chalice together, saying:

P: that they may become the Body and Blood of your Son our Lord Jesus Christ,

P: ut Corpus et Sanguis fiant Filii tui Domini nostri Iesu Christi,

He joins his hands.

P: at whose command we celebrate these mysteries.

P: cuius mandato haec mysteria celebramus.

For on the night he was betrayed

Ipse enim in qua nocte tradebatur

He takes the bread and, holding it slightly raised above the altar, continues:

P: he himself took bread, and, giving you thanks, he said the blessing, broke the bread and gave it to his disciples, saying:

P: accepit panem et tibi gratias agens benedixit, fregit, deditque discipulis suis, dicens:

He bows slightly

P: TAKE THIS, ALL OF YOU, AND EAT OF IT, FOR THIS IS MY BODY, WHICH WILL BE GIVEN UP FOR YOU.

P: ACCÍPITE ET MANDUCÁTE EX HOC OMNES: HOC EST ENIM CORPUS MEUM, QUOD PRO VOBIS TRADÉTUR.

He shows the consecrated host to the people, places it again on the paten, and genuflects in adoration. After this, he continues:

P: In a similar way, when supper was ended,

P: Símili modo, postquam cenátum est,

He takes the chalice and, holding it slightly raised above the altar,

P: he took the chalice, and, giving you thanks, he said the blessing, and gave the chalice to his disciples, saying:

P: accipiens calicem, et tibi gratias agens benedixit, deditque discipulis suis, dicens:

He bows slightly.

P: TAKE THIS, ALL OF YOU, AND DRINK FROM IT, FOR THIS IS THE CHALICE OF MY BLOOD, THE BLOOD OF THE NEW AND ETERNAL COVENANT, WHICH WILL BE POURED OUT FOR YOU AND FOR MANY FOR THE FORGIVENESS OF SINS. DO THIS IN MEMORY OF ME.

P: ACCÍPITE ET BÍBITE EX EO OMNES: HIC EST ENIM CALIX SÁNGUINIS MEI NOVI ET AETÉRNI TESTAMÉNTI, QUI PRO VOBIS ET PRO MULTIS EFFUNDÉTUR IN REMISSIÓN E M PECCATÓRUM. HOC FÁCITE IN MEAM COMMEMORATIÓNEM.

He shows the chalice to the people, places it on the corporal, and genuflects in adoration.

Then he says:

P: The mystery of faith.

C: We proclaim your Death, O Lord, and profess your Resurrection until you come again.

P: Mystérium fídei.

C: Mortem tuam annuntiámus, Dómine, et tuam resurrectiónem confitémur, donec vénias.

Vel:

Or:

When we eat this Bread and drink this Cup, we proclaim your Death, O Lord, until you come again.

Quotiescúmque manducámus panem hunc et cálicem bíbimus, mortem tuam annuntiámus, Dómine, donec vénias.

Vel:

Or:

Save us, Savior of the world, for by your Cross and Resurrection you have set us free.

Salvátor mundi, salva nos, qui per crucem et resurrectiónem tuam liberásti nos.

Then the Priest, with hands extended, says:

P: Therefore, O Lord, as we celebrate the memorial of the saving Passion of your Son, his wondrous Resurrection and Ascension into heaven, and as we look forward to his second coming, we offer you in thanksgiving this holy and living sacrifice.

P: Memores igitur, Domine, eiusdem Filii tui salutiferae passionis necnon mirabilis resurrectionis et ascensionis in caelum, sed et praestolantes alterum eius adventum, offerimus tibi, gratias referentes, hoc sacrificium vivum et sanctum.

Look, we pray, upon the oblation of your Church and, recognizing the sacrificial Victim by whose

Respice, quaesumus, in oblationem Ecclesiae tuae et, agnoscens Hostiam, cuius

death you willed to reconcile us to yourself, grant that we, who are nourished by the Body and Blood of your Son and filled with his Holy Spirit, may become one body, one spirit in Christ.

voluisti immolatione placari, concede, ut qui Corpore et Sanguine Filii tui reficimur, Spiritu eius Sancto repleti, unum corpus et unus spiritus inveniamur in Christo.

May he make of us an eternal offering to you, so that we may obtain an inheritance with your elect, especially with the most Blessed Virgin Mary, Mother of God, with your blessed Apostles and glorious Martyrs (with Saint N.: the Saint of the day or Patron Saint) and with all the Saints, on whose constant intercession in your presence we rely for unfailing help.

Ipse nos tibi perficiat munus aeternum, ut cum electis tuis hereditatem consequi valeamus, in primis cum beatissima Virgine, Dei Genetrice, Maria, cum beatis Apostolis tuis et gloriosis Martyribus et omnibus Sanctis, quorum intercessione perpetuo apud te confidimus adiuvari.

May this Sacrifice of our reconciliation, we pray, O Lord, advance the peace and salvation of all the world. Be pleased to

Haec Hostia nostrae reconciliationis proficiat, quaesumus, Domine, ad totius mundi pacem atque salutem.

confirm in faith and charity your pilgrim Church on earth, with your servant N. our Pope and N. our Bishop, the Order of Bishops, all the clergy, and the entire people you have gained for your own.

Listen graciously to the prayers of this family, whom you have summoned before you: in your compassion, O merciful Father, gather to yourself all your children scattered throughout the world.

Ecclesiam tuam, peregrinantem in terra, in fide et caritate firmare digneris cum famulo tuo Papa nostro N. et Episcopo nostro N., cum episcopali ordine et universo clero et omni populo acquisitionis tuae.

Votis huius familiae, quam tibi astare voluisti, adesto propitius. Omnes filios tuos ubique dispersos tibi, clemens Pater, miseratus coniunge.

To our departed brothers and sisters and to all who were pleasing to you at their passing from this life, give kind admittance to your kingdom. There we hope to enjoy for ever the fullness of your glory through Christ our Lord, through whom you bestow on the world all that is good.

Fratres nostros defunctos et omnes qui, tibi placentes, ex hoc saeculo transierunt, in regnum tuum benignus admitte, ubi fore speramus, ut simul gloria tua perenniter satiemur, per Christum Dominum nostrum, per quem mundo bona cuncta largiris.

He takes the chalice and the paten with the host and, raising both, he says:

P: Through him, and with him, and in him, O God, almighty Father, in the unity of the Holy Spirit, all glory and honor is yours, for ever and ever.

C: Amen.

P: Per ipsum, et cum ipso, et in ipso, est tibi Deo Patri omnipoténti, in unitáte Spíritus Sancti, omnis honor et glória per ómnia saecula saeculórum.

C: Amen.

Then follows the Communion Rite

EUCHARISTIC PRAYER IV

P: The Lord be with you.

C: And with your spirit.

P: Lift up your hearts.

C: We lift them up to the Lord.

P: Let us give thanks to the Lord our God.

C: It is right and just.

P: It is truly right to give you thanks, truly just to give you glory, Father most holy, for you are the one God living and true, existing before all ages and abiding for all eternity, dwelling in unapproachable light; yet you,

P: Dóminus vobíscum.

C: Et cum spíritu tuo.

P: Sursum corda.

C: Habémus ad Dóminum.

P: Grátias agámus Dómino Deo nostro.

C: Dignum et iustum est.

P: Vere dignum est tibi grátias ágere, vere iustum est te glorificáre, Pater sancte, quia unus es Deus vivus et verus, qui es ante saecula et pérmanes in aetérnum, inaccessíbilem lucem inhábitans; sed et qui unus bonus

who alone are good, the source of life, have made all that is, so that you might fill your creatures with blessings and bring joy to many of them by the glory of your light.

And so, in your presence are countless hosts of Angels, who serve you day and night and, gazing upon the glory of your face, glorify you without ceasing. With them we, too, confess your name in exultation, giving voice to every creature under heaven, as we acclaim:

C: Holy, Holy, Holy Lord God of hosts. Heaven and earth are full of your glory. Hosanna in the highest. Blessed is he who comes in the name of the Lord. Hosanna in the highest.

atque fons vitae cuncta fecísti, ut creatúras tuas benedictiónibus adimpléres multásque laetificáres tui lúminis claritáte.

Et ídeo coram te innúmerae astant turbae angelórum, qui die ac nocte sérviunt tibi et, vultus tui glóriam contemplántes, te incessánter gloríficant. Cum quibus et nos et, per nostram vocem, omnis quae sub caelo est creatúra nomen tuum in exsultatióne confitémur, canéntes:

C: Sanctus, Sanctus, Sanctus Dóminus Deus Sábaoth. Pleni sunt caeli et terra glória tua. Hosánna in excélsis. Benedíctus qui venit in nómine Dómini. Hosánna in excélsis.

The Priest, with hands extended, says:

P: We give you praise, Father

P: Confitémur tibi, Pater sancte,

most holy, for you are great and you have fashioned all your works in wisdom and in love. You formed man in your own image and entrusted the whole world to his care, so that in serving you alone, the Creator, he might have dominion over all creatures. And when through disobedience he had lost your friendship, you did not abandon him to the domain of death. For you came in mercy to the aid of all, so that those who seek might find you. Time and again you offered them covenants and through the prophets taught them to look forward to salvation.

And you so loved the world, Father most holy, that in the fullness of time you sent your Only Begotten Son to be our Savior. Made incarnate by the Holy Spirit and born of the

quia magnus es et ómnia ópera tua in sapiéntia et caritáte fecísti. Hóminem ad tuam imáginem condidísti, eíque commisísti mundi curam univérsi, ut, tibi soli Creatóri sérviens, creatúris ómnibus imperáret. Et cum amicítiam tuam, non oboédiens, amisísset, non eum dereliquísti in mortis império. Omnibus enim misericórditer subvenísti, ut te quaeréntes invenírent. Sed et foédera plúries homínibus obtulísti eósque per prophétas erudísti in exspectatióne salútis.

Et sic, Pater sancte, mundum dilexísti, ut, compléta plenitúdine témporum, Unigénitum tuum nobis mítteres Salvatórem. Qui, incarnátus de Spíritu Sancto et natus ex María

Virgin Mary, he shared our human nature in all things but sin. To the poor he proclaimed the good news of salvation, to prisoners, freedom, and to the sorrowful of heart, joy. To accomplish your plan, he gave himself up to death, and, rising from the dead, he destroyed death and restored life.

And that we might live no longer for ourselves but for him who died and rose again for us, he sent the Holy Spirit from you, Father, as the first fruits for those who believe, so that, bringing to perfection his work in the world, he might sanctify creation to the full.

He joins his hands and, holding them extended over the offerings, says:

P: Therefore, O Lord, we pray: may this same Holy Spirit graciously sanctify these

Vírgine, in nostra condiciónis forma est conversátus per ómnia absque peccáto; salútem evangelizávit paupéribus, redemptiónem captívis, maestis corde laetítiam. Ut tuam vero dispensatiónem impléret, in mortem trádidit semetípsum ac, resúrgens a mórtuis, mortem destrúxit vitámque renovávit.

Et, ut non ámplius nobismetípsis viverémus, sed sibi qui pro nobis mórtuus est atque surréxit, a te, Pater, misit Spíritum Sanctum primítias credéntibus, qui, opus suum in mundo perfíciens, omnem sanctificatiónem compléret.

P: Quaesumus ígitur, Dómine, ut idem Spíritus Sanctus haec múnera sanctificáre dignétur,

offerings,

He joins his hands and makes the Sign of the Cross once over the bread and chalice together, saying:

P: that they may become the Body and Blood of our Lord Jesus Christ

P: ut Corpus et Sanguis fiant Dómini nostri Iesu Christi

He joins his hands.

P: for the celebration of this great mystery, which he himself left us as an eternal covenant.

P: ad hoc magnum mystérium celebríndum, quod ipse nobis relíquit in fodus aetérnum

For when the hour had come for him to be glorified by you, Father most holy, having loved his own who were in the world, he loved them to the end: and while they were at supper,

Ipse enim, cum hora venísset ut glorificarétur a te, Pater sancte, ac dilexísset suos qui erant in mundo, in finem diléxit eos: et cenántibus illis,

He takes the bread and, holding it slightly raised above the altar, continues:

P: he took bread, blessed and broke it, and gave it to his disciples, saying,

P: accépit panem, benedíxit ac fregit, dedítque discípulis suis, dicens:

He bows slightly.

P: TAKE THIS, ALL OF YOU, AND EAT OF IT, FOR THIS IS

P: ACCÍPITE ET MANDUCÁTE EX HOC

MY BODY, WHICH WILL BE GIVEN UP FOR YOU.

OMNES: HOC EST ENIM CORPUS MEUM, QUOD PRO VOBIS TRADÉTUR.

He shows the consecrated host to the people, places it again on the paten, and genuflects in adoration.

After this, he continues:

P: In a similar way,

P: Símili modo accipit calicem,

He takes the chalice and, holding it slightly raised above the altar, continues:

P: taking the chalice filled with the fruit of the vine, he gave thanks, and gave the chalice to his disciples, saying:

P: accípiens cálicem, ex genímine vitis replétum, grátias egit, dedítque discípulis suis, dicens:

He bows slightly.

P: TAKE THIS, ALL OF YOU, AND DRINK FROM IT, FOR THIS IS THE CHALICE OF MY BLOOD, THE BLOOD OF THE NEW AND ETERNAL COVENANT, WHICH WILL BE POURED OUT FOR YOU AND FOR MANY FOR THE FORGIVENESS OF SINS. DO THIS IN MEMORY OF ME.

P: ACCÍPITE ET BÍBITE EX EO OMNES: HIC EST ENIM CALIX SÁNGUINIS MEI NOVI ET AETÉRNI TESTAMÉNTI, QUI PRO VOBIS ET PRO MULTIS EFFUNDÉTUR IN REMISSIÓNEM PECCATÓRUM. HOC FÁCITE IN MEAM COMMEMORATIÓNEM.

P: The mystery of faith.

C: We proclaim your Death, O Lord, and profess your Resurrection until you come again.

Or:

When we eat this Bread and drink this Cup, we proclaim your Death, O Lord, until you come again.

Or:

Save us, Savior of the world, for by your Cross and Resurrection you have set us free.

P: Mystérium fídei.

C: Mortem tuam annuntiámus Dómine, et tuam resurrectiónem confitémur, donec vénias.

Vel:

Quotiescúmque manducámus panem hunc et cálicem bíbimus, mortem tuam annuntiámus, Dómine, donec vénias.

Vel:

Salvátor mundi, salva nos, qui per crucem et resurrectiónem tuam liberásti nos.

Then, with hands extended, the Priest says:

P: Therefore, O Lord, as we now celebrate the memorial of our redemption, we remember Christ's Death and his descent to the realm of the dead, we

P: Unde et nos, Dómine, redemptiónis nostrae memoriále nunc celebrántes, mortem Christi eiúsque descénsum ad ínferos recólimus, eius resurrectiónem et

proclaim his Resurrection and his Ascension to your right hand, and, as we await his coming in glory, we offer you his Body and Blood, the sacrifice acceptable to you which brings salvation to the whole world.

ascensiónem ad tuam déxteram profitémur, et, exspectántes ipsíus advéntum in glória, offérimus tibi eius Corpus et Sánguinem, sacrifícium tibi acceptábile et toti mundo salutáre.

Look, O Lord, upon the Sacrifice which you yourself have provided for your Church, and grant in your loving kindness to all who partake of this one Bread and one Chalice that, gathered into one body by the Holy Spirit, they may truly become a living sacrifice in Christ to the praise of your glory.

Réspice, Dómine, in Hóstiam, quam Ecclésiae tuae ipse parásti, et concéde benígnus omnibus qui ex hoc uno pane participábunt et cálice, ut, in unum corpus a Sancto Spíritu congregáti, in Christo hóstia viva perficiántur, ad laudem glóriae tuae.

Therefore, Lord, remember now all for whom we offer this sacrifice: especially your servant N. our Pope, N. our Bishop, and the whole Order of Bishops, all the clergy, those who take part in

Nunc ergo, Dómine, ómnium recordáre, pro quibus tibi hanc oblatiónem offérimus: in primis fámuli tui, Papae nostril N., Epíscopi nostril N. et Episcopórum órdinis univérsi,

this offering, those gathered here before you, your entire people, and all who seek you with a sincere heart.

Remember also those who have died in the peace of your Christ and all the dead, whose faith you alone have known. To all of us, your children, grant, O merciful Father, that we may enter into a heavenly inheritance with the Blessed Virgin Mary, Mother of God, and with your Apostles and Saints in your kingdom. There, with the whole of creation, freed from the corruption of sin and death, may we glorify you through Christ our Lord, through whom you bestow on the world all that is good.

sed et totíus cleri, et offeréntium, et circumstántium, et cuncti pópuli tui, et ómnium, qui te quaerunt corde sincéro.

Meménto étiam illórum, qui obiérunt in pace Christi tui, et ómnium defunctórum, quorum fidem tu solus cognovísti. Nobis ómnibus, fíliis tuis, clemens Pater, concéde, ut caeléstem hereditátem cónsequi valeámus cum beáta Vírgine, Dei Genetríce, María, cum beáto Ioseph, eius Sponso, cum Apóstolis et Sanctis tuis in regno tuo, ubi cum univérsa creatúra, a corruptióne peccáti et mortis liberáta, te glorificémus per Christum Dóminum nostrum, per quem mundo bona cuncta largíris.

He takes the chalice and the paten with the host and, raising both, he says:

P: Through him, and with him,

P: Per ipsum, et cum ipso, et in

45

and in him, O God, almighty Father, in the unity of the Holy Spirit, all glory and honor is yours, for ever and ever.

C: Amen.

ipso, est tibi Deo Patri omnipoténti, in unitáte Spíritus Sancti, omnis honor et glória per ómnia saecula saeculórum.

C: Amen.

Then follows the Communion Rite.

The Communion Rite

After the chalice and paten have been set down, the Priest, with hands joined, says:

P: At the Savior's command and formed by divine teaching, we dare to say:

P: Præcéptis salutáribus móniti, et divína institutióne formáti, audémus dícere:

He extends his hands and, together with the people, continues:

Our Father, who art in heaven, hallowed be thy name; thy kingdom come, thy will be done on earth as it is in heaven. Give us this day our daily bread, and forgive us our trespasses, as we forgive those who trespass against us; and lead us not into temptation, but deliver us from evil.

Pater noster, qui es in caelis: sanctificetur nomen tuum; adveniat regnum tuum; fiat voluntas tua, sicut in caelo, et in terra. Panem nostrum cotidianum da nobis hodie; et dimitte nobis debita nostra, sicutet nos dimittimus debitoribus nostris; et ne nos inducas in tentationem; sed libera nos a malo.

P: Deliver us, Lord, we pray, from every evil, graciously grant peace in our days, that, by the help of your mercy, we may be always free from sin and safe from all distress, as we await the blessed hope and the coming of our Savior, Jesus Christ.

P: Libera nos, quaesumus, Domine, ab omnibus malis, da propitius pacem in diebus nostris, ut, ope misericordiae tuae adiuti, et a peccato simus semper liberi et ab omni perturbatione securi: exspectantes beatam spem et adventum Salvatoris nostri Iesu Christi.

He joins his hands.

And the people conclude the prayer, acclaiming:

C: For the kingdom, the power and the glory are yours now and forever.

C: Quia tuum est regnum, et potestas, et Gloria in saecula.

Then the Priest, with hands extended, says aloud:

P: Lord Jesus Christ, who said to your Apostles: Peace I leave you, my peace I give you; look not on our sins, but on the faith of your Church, and graciously grant her peace and unity in accordance with your will. Who live and reign for ever and ever.

P: Domine Iesu Christe, qui dixisti Apostolis tuis: Pacem relinquo vobis, pacem meam do vobis: ne respicias peccata nostra, sed fidem Ecclesiae tuae; eamque secundum voluntatem tuam pacificare et coadunare digneris. Qui vivis et regnas in saecula saeculorum.

C: Amen.   C: Amen.

The Priest, turned towards the people, extending and then joining his hands, adds:

P: The peace of the Lord be   P: Pax Dómini sit semper
with you always.   vobíscum.

C: And with your spirit.   C: Et cum spíritu tuo.

P: Let us offer each other the   P: Offérte vobis pacem.
sign of peace.

BREAKING OF THE BREAD

Meanwhile the following is sung or said:

Lamb of God, you take away   Agnus Dei, qui tollis peccata
the sins of the world: Have   mundi: miserere nobis.
mercy on us.   Agnus Dei, qui tollis peccata
Lamb of God, you take away   mundi: miserere nobis.
the sins of the world: Have   Agnus Dei, qui tollis peccata
mercy on us.   mundi: dona nobis pacem.
Lamb of God, you take away
the sins of the world: Grant us
peace.

Then the Priest, with hands joined, says quietly:

P: Lord Jesus Christ, Son of   P: Domine Iesu Christe, Fili
the living God, who, by the   Dei vivi, qui ex voluntate
will of the Father and the work   Patris, cooperante Spiritu

of the Holy Spirit, through your Death gave life to the world, free me by this, your most holy Body and Blood, from all my sins and from every evil; keep me always faithful to your commandments, and never let me be parted from you.

Sancto, per mortem tuam mundum vivificasti: libera me per hoc sacrosanctum Corpus et Sanguinem tuum ab omnibus iniquitatibus meis et universis malis: et fac me tuis semper inhaerere mandatis, et a te numquam separari permittas.

Or:

Vel:

P: May the receiving of your Body and Blood, Lord Jesus Christ, not bring me to judgement and condemnation, but through your loving mercy be for me protection in mind and body and a healing remedy.

P: Perceptio Corporis et Sanguinis tui, Domine Iesu Christe, non mihi proveniat in iudicium et condemnationem: sed pro tua pietate prosit mihi ad tutamentum mentis et corporis, et ad medelam percipiendam.

The Priest genuflects, takes the host and, holding it slightly raised above the paten or above the chalice, while facing the people, says aloud:

P: Behold the Lamb of God, Behold him who takes away the sins of the world. Blessed are those called to the supper of the Lamb.

P: Ecce Agnus Dei, ecce qui tollit peccata mundi. Beati qui ad cenam Agni vocati sunt.

C: Lord, I am not worthy that you should enter under my roof, But only say the word and my soul shall be healed.

C: Domine, non sum dignus, ut intres sub tectum meum: sed tantum dic verbo, et sanabitur anima mea.

The Priest, facing the altar, says quietly:

P: May the Body of Christ keep me safe for eternal life.

P: Corpus Christi custódiat me in vitam ætérnam.

And he reverently consumes the Body of Christ. Then he takes the chalice and says quietly:

P: May the Blood of Christ keep me safe for eternal life.

P: Sanguis Christi custódiat me in vitam ætérnam.

And he reverently consumes the Blood of Christ.

COMMUNION

After this, he takes the paten or ciborium and approaches the communicants. The Priest raises a host slightly and shows it to each of the communicants, saying:

P: The Body of Christ.

P: Corpus Christi.

The communicant replies:

C: Amen.

C: Amen.

(And receives Holy Communion)

PRAYER AFTER COMMUNION

When the distribution of Communion is over, the Priest or a Deacon or an acolyte purifies the paten over the chalice and also the chalice itself. While he carries out the purification, the Priest

says quietly:

P: What has passed our lips as food, O Lord, may we possess in purity of heart, that what has been given to us in time may be our healing for eternity.

P: Quod ore súmpsimus, Dómine, pura mente capiámus, et de múnere temporáli fiat nobis remédium sempitérnum.

Then, standing at the altar or at the chair and facing the people, with hands joined, the Priest says:

P: Let us pray.

P: Orémus.

The Priest, with hands extended, says the Prayer after Communion, at the end of which the people acclaim:

C: Amen.

C: Amen.

The Concluding Rites

The Priest, facing the people and extending his hands, says:

P: The Lord be with you.

P: Dominus vobiscum.

C: And with your spirit.

C: Et cum spiritu tuo.

P: May almighty God bless you, the Father, and the Son, and the Holy Spirit.

P: Benedícat vos omnípotens Deus, May almighty God bless you: Pater, et Filius, et Spíritus the Father, and the Son, and Sanctus.

C: Amen.

C: Amen.

DISMISSAL

Then the Deacon, or the Priest himself, with hands joined and facing the people, says:

P: Go forth, the Mass is ended.

P: Ite, missa est.

Or:

Vel:

P: Go and announce the Gospel of the Lord.

P: Ite ad Evangelium Domini nuntiandum.

Or:

Vel:

P: Go in peace, glorifying the Lord by your life.

P: Ite in pace, glorificando vita vestra Dominum.

Or:

Vel:

P: Go in peace.

P: vade in pace

C: Thanks be to God.

C: Deo gratias.

The congregation remains standing until the priest and the procession have left the church.

Made in the USA
Las Vegas, NV
17 December 2024